CW00819502

The Satanic Narratives
A Modern Satanic Bible

TRACEY PRYOR
12/15/14

Damien Ba'al

Published by HLA Publishing LLC

Copyright © 2015 by Damien Ba'al
 Published in Hell by HLA Publishing LLC
hlapublishing.com
ISBN: 978-0-9968101-0-4

To outcasts and individualists everywhere.
You are never alone.

Acknowledgements

Very special thanks to Wendy Ba'al for her love and support.

Thanks to Wendy Ba'al, Greg Stevens, and Lilith Starr for giving me so much help and support in the process of revising this book.

Thanks to Iris Shaw for the cover art.

Thanks to Tracey Pryor for the title page art, and the sigil of Baphomet.

Print layout time donated by The First Church of Satan, Amarillo TX, Order of The Garthok

Thanks to Khandnalie Barnes for all other sigils and symbols.

Thanks to Xen Darens for photo editing.

Thanks to Malcolm Jarry and Doug Mesner for presenting Satanism in a new, dark, infernal light.

A special posthumous acknowledgment of thanks to Anton Szandor LaVey for his great and numerous contributions to Satanism.

Table Of Contents

Satanism, as a religion, philosophy, and worldview, acts as a summation of all aspects of who I am. This is the first of two primary reasons for the existence of this textual actualization of foundational Satanic philosophy. The other reason prompting me to start writing is much more basic, ordinary, and practical. There simply is not a book of this sort yet in existence. There are numerous similar books, but nothing that expresses my particular variation of Satanism.

Satanism combines a number of different things into one—or at least some variations do. My variation is all-encompassing. It incorporates philosophies for understanding objective reality, subjective experience, morality and ethics, and even my personality.

There is also a lack of quality Satanic philosophy. The book most people identify with, The Satanic Bible, has its good points, but it is also outdated and full of flaws. Anton Szandor LaVey had a few good ideas, which were never utilized to their full potential. He also had a lot of bad ideas, and poor execution, which held him back.

Those problems can be corrected. There is much that

we now know that was not known back in the 1960's. The original Satanic Bible can be improved both philosophically and linguistically. The dreadful misunderstanding of natural selection can also be corrected by incorporating selection by group survival and our status as a social species. It was this misunderstanding by LaVey, Rand, and Redbeard, which resulted in the social Darwinism that permeated their philosophies.

Their idea was that the natural world was the only place to look for secular morality. Their understanding of natural selection was that the strongest and fittest on an individual level are the ones that survive. However, they overlooked species that had survival mechanisms built into their social structure. Humans are one such species that fall into this category. I offer a superior implementation of secular morality, in part by correcting this oversight.

I begin with some of LaVey's ideas as a starting point, but the similarity will end there. Other than ideas about Satan as the adversary, looking to the natural world for the origins of our being, and understanding and accepting humanity as it is, this will be very different.

I am not saying this is the only true Satanism. There are only a few basic ideas that are definitive of Satanism in all its variations. This is just my variation, and I provide reasons why it resonates with me. So, read on, take in and consider the information presented, and see if it resonates with you as well.

Ave Satanas!

Introduction to Satan

The first thing to understand regarding Satanism is that the stories of sacrificial alters, secret cults of evil, and brutal ritualized abuse are categorically false. Those ideas came from a moral panic in the 80's and 90's, commonly referred to as the "Satanic Panic".

The Satanic Panic was a modern witch-hunt that some people still believe to this day. The rise of Christian culture, the (then) new psychological fraud of so-called "recovered memories", and the nature of the general public as a herd of witless, scared sheep gave rise to it. Its negative effects still linger, even now. It is the primary source of the bigotry faced by Satanists.

Looking back on it, we have decades of lies and deception. Paranoia ran rampant, obscuring truth and reason. Talk shows did numerous exposés over many years, each fantastical and totally devoid of fact checking. Countless lives were ruined as false accusations sent the innocent to prison, and targeted many others for completely benign beliefs.

I know I have just scratched the surface with that

topic. However, digging in further would be tangential and out of scope for this book. It did need to be mentioned though.

The next thing to understand is that Satan is not an actual being. Satan does not literally exist. There are theists who believe in that sort of thing, but I do not. This is actually an atheistic religion and philosophy. Satan is just a metaphorical construct that symbolizes certain ideals. There are different aspects of Satan, which all give characteristics to the archetype.

You can see the Satan archetype come to life in classic literature, such as Milton's "Paradise Lost" and "Revolt of the Angels" by Anatole France. Mythology is another good place to look, and in fact, that is where the characteristics of the literary Satan were drawn from.

Different demonized (literally) gods became aspects of Satan, shaping this mythological character. I will divide most of this book by categorizing certain ideas by the aspect of Satan, with which they are associated. The ideas will make logical sense on their own, independent of these archetypes though. This is merely a way to organize the information and simultaneously demonstrate the metaphorical construct.

Some people use Satanism as an excuse to be an ass. It is very reminiscent of people who use an Abrahamic religion as an excuse to be a bigot. Justification of lousy behavior, and personal shortcomings, while blindly quoting some document you follow unquestioningly is of traditional religion. The Satanist is in diametrical opposition to such nonsense.

Think of me as a teacher, advisor, or guide and not so much as a leader. The Satanist does not really need a leader per say. I lead only metaphorically, guiding one through philosophical concepts. I offer what knowledge and wisdom I have, but you must lead yourself. Myself and others can help you, and we will, but this is your journey. You must push yourself through it, and you reap the rewards along the way, down the path; the Left-Hand Path.

The Narrative of Satan

Satan literally means "adversary". Satan is primarily opposition and rebellion. It is the unbowed will in the face of oppression, the eternal rebel versus the ultimate dictator. It is an unrelenting rebellion waged against the antitheses of Satanic ideals and deeply held beliefs.

This says nothing of what the ideals and beliefs are, as that will be covered later. This is simply a call to action, and is the root of the Satan archetype. It can be done in one's own name, or in the defense of other people.

Because of this, the Satanist must have some involvement in activism. While the Satanist does take time to thoroughly enjoy life, (as you will read about later), they do not remain idle in the shadow of oppression and injustice. Satan is opposition to such things, and one must be the adversary.

Take care not to confuse or pollute these ideas with untenable concepts like vengeance and retribution. Such things are a pointless and often destructive form of overindulgence in catharsis. The adversary should have a purpose, and accomplish something, not neglect one's critical thought to engage in the primitive savagery of the mindless populace.

When one indulges in cathartic emotion, it should never be at the expense of one's force of opposition or of other Satanic ideals. Let it be measured, let it serve a purpose, let it be done in the light of reason. Only then is the Satanist truly the adversary.

Traditional religion is one of the main things to which the Satanist stands in opposition. There are very good reasons this is the case too. First is the sheep-like nature in which the people are indoctrinated and led around in a herd. Next is the willful ignorance—they hold onto superstition, fantasy, and delusion as tight as they can, while rejecting contrary knowledge no matter how much evidence supports it. Frequently their moral compass is spinning out of control, too, as their poisonous delusion pulls at the needle, leaving them twisted.

They are made to believe they cannot behave without their imaginary friend watching over them. Some of them set out to demonstrate this too. They feel they have no purpose without this magic father in the sky, and their leaders make it so they are too weak willed to have any purpose other than being steered like a herd of tranquilized cattle. Looking to an imaginary paradise, which will never come, they pledge their real lives to slavery, keeping themselves captive.

The Satanist is free of such things, and takes delight in mocking the ridiculous ideas, and taking joy in breaking their rules. However, at the same time, the Satanist has pity on the people. How can one feel anything else for a fellow human who has been enslaved, stuck in a trap sprung on them when they were too young to think? Cruelty is for the leaders of these slaves, and they dish it out regularly. The Satanist stands in opposition to this. Cruelty, ignorance, slavery, and the people steeped in such things—we are your adversary.

The Narrative of Ba'al

Ba'al is the outcast, the outsider, the hated other, and the one who perseveres. The Lord of the Sky was demonized and renamed the Lord of Flies. The implication being that he was a piece of shit. Ba'al, Baal, Bel, or other variations simply translated as "lord". Therefore, there were many mythological beings that could be called Ba'al, and no doubt, many were demonized. This is about the Lord of Flies though, Ba'al Zebub, who is best known as Beelzebub.

The Satanist, who will likely be eccentric in nature and unconventional in behavior, is usually in some way, the outcast. The Satanist embraces this outsider status. As an adversary, one should be content to be the hated other in some situations and circumstances.

The Satanist does not need the approval or validation of the masses. Instead, one should persevere in the face of opposition as the hated other. This is not to dismiss community and companionship, which will be covered later, but simply that it matters from whom those things come. The docile, unthinking masses of the general populace is not the source of such things. Therefore, let yourself bask in their disapproval, soak it in, do not take it to heart, but let it nourish you. This adds to the energy reserves fueling one's perseverance—a quality much needed by the adversary.

Look around you for these hated others, these outcasts, for they are likely your brothers and sisters in opposition. They may not know it, but they will learn in time. Such people are likely on the Left-Hand Path. You may do well to welcome them. From these you may find loyal and powerful allies to aide you in your adversarial pursuits.

The Left-Hand Path and Satanic aspects of one's personality, lead to being the outsider, and when one embraces their outcast status, it magnifies the attraction to this religion and philosophy. Therefore, it is both a cause and effect, each magnifying the other.

When you open your eyes, and look around you, you see you are not the only one cast out of society. With the light of reason no longer obscured by a mass collective of the docile and credulous, you can see the arbitrary social conventions, norms, and roles, for the irrational, detrimental things that they are.

Then it is with feelings of relief and exhilaration, that you realize you have been liberated rather than cast out. The grass is greener where you now stand. You feel only sorrow for the people on the inside, trapped in a mental prison of their own social construction.

The Narrative of Lucifer

Of all the aspects of Satan, we get the most from Lucifer. Lucifer is the bringer of light, wisdom, and knowledge. The intellectual focus, critical thinking skills, and the valuing of human beings come from this aspect. The literary Satan is very Luciferian.

Scientific and philosophical skepticism are the most accurate way to understand objective reality. This includes our best understanding of modern science as well as cogent, logical arguments.

As an atheistic form of Satanism, this skepticism is applied to the concept of gods. There is no evidence for any gods, therefore no reason to believe in any. There is no reason to give a moment's consideration to any unfalsifiable, presupposed being for whom there is no existential evidence. Without a logical argument or empirical data, there is no way one could know of the concept of any god without someone having made it up. The only other source of firsthand knowledge would be the mind, and therefore the idea is a fabrication.

One could postulate a universe with no gods, demons,

etc. and that universe would be identical to the one we occupy. Humans have invented countless imaginary beings, and all leave no trace of existence in our reality. The god concept truly is a ridiculous philosophical proposition.

When one applies this skepticism to the supernatural in general, the resultant yield is identical. Supernaturalism is therefore rejected on this same total lack of evidence. There are some things that are logically impossible, and we can be certain such things do not exist, or such propositions are not true. However, some things cannot be falsified at all. In that case, we lack knowledge of it. That results in a lack of belief in that thing.

Lacking knowledge is to be agnostic. One is agnostic in regard to an unfalsifiable being for which there is no evidence, but not in regard to a logically impossible being. The result on belief is the same though. One does not believe it.

Belief is a binary state. Either you believe something or you do not. Knowledge is a separate question altogether. Even if you do not know whether you do or do not believe something, you do, in fact, either believe or not believe. That is the nature of belief.

Therefore, if you are not a theist, you would be an atheist. You believe or you do not. For most concepts of supernatural beings, you would also lack knowledge, and therefore be agnostic as well.

This requirement for preexisting evidence should be a prerequisite for all knowledge. The philosophical and scientific skeptic believes no objective statement of any significance without reason or empirical evidence. This is the beginning of knowledge and wisdom. The Lucifer aspect of Satan symbolizes these ideals of Satanism.

The Satanist should have a love of learning, exploration, and discovery. These things allow one to continue to gain knowledge and wisdom. Such intellectual fortitude will serve you well.

The Lucifer character was something of a Humanist. He placed a lot of value on human beings. This is only the beginning of morality though, and as such, that topic will be covered in the next narrative. This focus on people, in regard to this Satanic aspect, will take the form of sharing knowledge and wisdom.

The sharing and proliferation of knowledge and wisdom is another Satanic ideal. One should teach what one knows to any person willing to learn. Knowledge, wisdom, and critical thinking skills are the greatest gift one can give.

Not everyone is ready to learn, let them come to you when the time is right. Some people are not willing to learn, and are not worth the effort. Through learning, the ignorant and irrational can be turned into reasonable people with an adequate understanding. The less of the former and the more of the latter, the better your world and life experience will be. Everyone wins.

This life is the only one there is. Make the most of it. Everything you are is simply an incredibly complex array of chemical reactions and electrical impulses in the brain. This gives rise to your consciousness and self-awareness. When the brain dies, this process stops, and the person no longer exists.

Not only are heaven, hell and afterlife myths, but dualism is as well. There is no soul or spirit, your mind is one entity, and it is merely the way you experience reality. You are your mind, and the narrative of subjective experience this mind constructs from all of the input received, is your life. All of this is just physical processes that are part of the normal functioning of the brain. Each piece had an evolutionary advantage, and put together, they result in the essence of human beings.

The Narrative of Baphomet

Baphomet symbolizes balance, human nature, and the natural world. The human-centric focus of Lucifer works in conjunction with this to give us a robust, naturalist morality, with a proper basis for our normative values.

Balance, in the context of Baphomet, shows us two opposing extreme opposites. The meaning is that these two things are not the only choices—a whole infinity of gray may exist between them, and frequently the two extremes do not exist at all. Good and evil do not really exist in the way they are used as a label on people. Thought and behavior is a mix of these things, too scrambled to isolate a definitive "good" or a definitive "evil".

There is a school of thought that one should turn the other cheek when wronged. Another that says you should not, but instead you should exact vengeance and retribution. This is a false dichotomy. Furthermore, either option is highly illogical and asserts meaning on concepts, which are tenuous at best.

Forgiveness can be a wonderful thing, but exposing oneself to the risk of further negative events is highly irrational. There is no reason why you must follow the other one either. Vengeance and retribution are meaningless concepts invoked by primitive savages, usually in the context of superstition. They solve nothing, and are merely an indulgence in catharsis. There is not anything inherently wrong with this catharsis, but many fool themselves into thinking it accomplishes something other than stroking one's emotions. It is sometimes counter-productive. You may burn a bridge you will need to cross, and your emotional indulgence can work against you if you are not careful.

The nature of reality is: Shit Happens. Many events are largely beyond one's control. There is no intentionality guiding anything. We are adrift in a chaotic universe, like a raft with no rudder or paddles, flowing through different currents, winds blowing us in different directions. One can exert a certain amount of influence, and accomplish things, but life is not fair, and a great many things are beyond one's control.

The universe has no objective moral code, and without that or any gods, there can be no truly objective morality. At this level, nothing matters, and no outcome is better than any other. Morality begins at this place of nihilism and chaos.

We must have some sort of basis for our morality, for the value judgments we make. Many people looked to nature to do this, and that is certainly the right direction, but it is not so simple. The problem with ideas like survival of the fit and strong is it assumes a fairness that simply cannot exist in this chaotic reality. It also ignores the group survival advantage, which is critical to natural selection in any social species such as humans. Finally, it tries to make a value judgment, or assert the way something should be, based only on what is.

The existence of something in nature contains no information regarding how that thing should be.

The group survival aspect that is ignored can be made a focal point. This action also solves the other two problems. Understanding that we are a social species, and we evolved to survive as a group, is critically important. Surviving as a group allows us collectively to compensate for negative events that happen in our chaotic reality.

It also gives us something we call a conscience. This is what we call our raw moral feelings. As a social species, we have these feelings in common, as they are a product of our evolution. They are subjective as they are feelings, but because we all have them, we can treat them as if they were objective. It is kind of like every single person liking chocolate ice cream the best. Chocolate would not objectively be the best flavor, as it is a subjective experience, but being universal would mean it could be treated exactly the same as something that is an objective fact.

This is the basis and beginning of morality. We can use logic, reason, and empirical evidence to shape and improve this morality. However, at the same time illogic, superstition, ignorance, and good old-fashioned stupidity can corrupt one's moral compass.

We can also use reason to decide on actions we should take based on these moral feelings. So while it starts with a feeling, it being virtually universal allows it to be treated the same as something objective. Reason and empirical evidence are objective. Therefore, you can have a sense of what is more right, and what is less right. This highlights where on the spectrum something is, as far as how positive or negative its effects would be.

This brings us to an understanding, where we can have certain moral truths. These truths can be expressed in a code of ethics. These statements of morality are fundamental and cover the vast majority of situations. However, the fundamental nature of any list of moral precepts can never be applied to everything. Sometimes additional reasoning is required.

Secular ethics is the branch of moral philosophy one would use to construct a secular moral code. It is based on the ideas explained up to this point, and gives guidelines for a certain formulaic way of crafting a code of ethics. The main points of the formula for creating a set of secular ethics are covering all the basic concepts, keeping each one brief, and having a poetic feel to it. I decided for a couple different reasons to endorse an existing code of secular ethics rather than create my own.

If I did make a code of ethics, it would look like a copy of other codes because of the formulaic nature. If I tried to move away from the formula to make it different, it would not turn out well at all. That is why the formula is always followed when creating these. In addition, there is no need to reinvent the wheel.

Since there is a code of secular ethics well known to many Satanists, and I happen to think it is a particularly well-crafted one, I decided to endorse that set of moral tenets. This code of secular ethics is called, "The Seven Tenets", and is well known as the central piece of philosophy of the religious organization called, "The Satanic Temple".

Doug Mesner, who also goes by the name Lucien Greaves, wrote The Seven Tenets and cofounded The Satanic Temple. I will print their tenets here for your convenience.

20

As you will see, it follows the formula for secular ethics perfectly, and is linguistically beautiful.

1)   One should strive to act with compassion and empathy towards all creatures in accordance with reason.

2)   The struggle for justice is an ongoing and necessary pursuit that should prevail over laws and institutions.

3)   One's body is inviolable, subject to one's own will alone.

4)   The freedoms of others should be respected, including the freedom to offend. To willfully and unjustly encroach upon the freedoms of another is to forgo your own.

5)   Beliefs should conform to our best scientific understanding of the world. We should take care never to distort scientific facts to fit our beliefs.

6)   People are fallible. If we make a mistake, we should do our best to rectify it and resolve any harm that may have been caused.

7)   Every tenet is a guiding principle designed to inspire nobility in action and thought. The spirit of compassion, wisdom, and justice should always prevail over the written or spoken word.

The Narrative of The Leviathan

The Leviathan symbolizes life, health, community, and creativity. The first two things are fairly self-explanatory. It is the other two that will be the focus. Community, and our instinct to live that way, come from our evolution as a social species. A group of like-minded individuals can find mutual benefit in association. The sharing of the joys of life with companions makes those moments all the more sweet. Sometimes you might find yourself doing things to help others, but when you need it, you should find these others coming to your aid.

Even the most independent and individualistic people need allies and a support system. You do not want to be the outcast by yourself, and you cannot affect as much change if you are the lone adversary. Community can help in your endeavors, and allow you to be a part of the interesting activities others might be planning.

Community should be individuals who happen to have converging interests and goals. They should never be a collective of sheep blindly following for no reason other than to follow. There is a large and important difference there. One is Satanic. The other is slavery.

23

Creativity is another important thing. Even people who do not see themselves as creative will be good at something. The Satanist should find what they are good at, and refine that skill. Having something one is good at gives one a sense of accomplishment and purpose. It is also one of those pleasures of life, which call out for our indulgence.

With a community of people who all have at least some sort of creative ability, those abilities can be combined to do amazing things. It is kind of like the concept of emergence, where you end up with something that is more than the sum of its parts. Like the brain, for example. It is just made up of cells, and none of the cells have any conscious thought, but put together as they are, it results in the existence of a conscious mind.

Through communal emergence, you can create a very a powerful adversary. One that can bend the world, just a little, to the desire of your will. One that can affect change to a greater extent than could any one person. It is the closest thing there is to magic. Its power is limited only by the community and their combined creative energies.

Ceremonies and celebrations are a great thing for a community to have. I created a set of ceremonies. I had written them out, mostly as customizable templates, but I never was completely happy with them. I think the reason is that if any of it is prewritten, it loses the personal meaning it should have. Writing specifics should be up to the Satanic priest or other practitioner, and the person or persons involved. With my following explanation, you should be able to make your own.

With all of these, you decide exactly what is said, how it goes, if there is ritual involved, and if so, what that ritual is.

I have seven of them, which I call the Seven Satanic Ceremonies.

The Announcing is for an expectant woman or couple. It is a very special time for individuals who decide to have children, and should be acknowledged.

The Welcoming is when a new person is welcomed to the world, and the caregivers pledge to do their best.

The Transitioning marks the end of childhood and the beginning of adolescence, around the age of thirteen. This is a time of more freedom, and more responsibility. It also marks the beginning of a difficult time in the lives of most people.

The Becoming is when you reach physical adulthood at eighteen. However, it never really ends until your life does. You are always becoming a better person than you were the day before, as you travel the Left-Hand Path. The Joining is for welcoming and initiating new members. It can be as simple or elaborate, as you want.

The Wedding can be anything you want. Consenting adults are the only prerequisite.

The Ending is like a funeral. It is a celebration of the life, which recently ended. It is also a final farewell, but mostly it is about celebrating and commemorating a life.

How one does this, or if one does any of them at all, is up to the individual. These are just here in case you want to create your own in this format. Ultimately, you decide what works best for you.

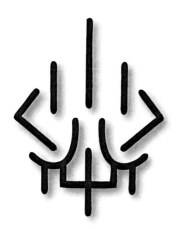

The Narrative of Belial

Belial symbolizes individualism, independence and accomplishment. This aspect is an animated and anthropomorphized representation of the Left-Hand Path. This path is about the discovery, acceptance, and fulfillment of self.

Though it might seem a paradox, individualism and independence are actually critical traits to have in members of any community. This leads to accomplishment, and only through these individual accomplishments, do we get the emergence mentioned in the previous section.

Being an individual, thinking for yourself, and refusing to blindly follow are critically important and definitive traits of Satanism. It should be pointed out that this is different from stubbornness and contrarianism. Being a reverse sheep really is not any better than being a regular sheep.

The Left-Hand Path is sometimes viewed as selfish, or some even portray it that way when they hold selfishness up as a virtue. This simply is not true. You must love yourself before you can love others, and you must provide for your own needs before you can do so for anyone else.

Taking a little time for yourself is a matter of health and sanity. Everyone needs that. You are the foundation of your world. Without caring for yourself, everything you are doing will eventually come crashing down.

Accomplishment is important, and it is the fruit of creativity. The creativity each person hones leads to each person having some sort of accomplishment. Every Satanist should have something they have done, something in which to take pride, something that brings satisfaction. If everyone in a community is a strong willed, creative individualist with notable accomplishments, your emergent power would be quite a formidable adversary indeed.

Accomplishment is also part of fulfillment. This fulfillment of self is the essence of the Left-Hand Path. It brings one joy, and a sort of inner peace.

Frequently touted in Satanism is the idea of worshiping oneself as a god. I do not like that though. Neither concept—not god, nor worship, is worthy even of acknowledgement. They are both silly ideas, for which I have nothing but contempt. Unless you are using the word "god" in the context of mythology or euphemism, it is in no way an accurate label for anything.

Worship is the same way. What an utterly ridiculous thing to do. Unless you are using it in the context of BDSM or in some other sexual way, it is a way of thinking and a behavior, which is nothing but shameful.

There is nothing wrong with considering yourself to be the most important entity in existence. However, even the most important thing ever is not a god, and it does not warrant worship. I think such words are best left to the traditionally religious, as they do one of those concepts to the other, which also happens to be imaginary. What being would want worship anyway? I do not think much of anything that wants constant over-the-top adoration.

Instead, simply develop love and respect for yourself. This should happen if you follow the Left-Hand Path. If you have trouble with it, do things to become a better person. That makes it easier. It is also good to have some personal growth on this journey, and it is part of self-fulfillment, which is central to the Left-Hand Path.

The Narrative of Pan

Pan symbolizes indulgence, hedonism, sex, music, drink, food, celebrations—everything that makes life fun and enjoyable. Traditional religions view all these things as evil. It is the exact opposite for the Satanist. There is nothing to be gained from deprivation. It is not inherently virtuous. Indulgence and making the most of this one life that you have is the thing that is truly virtuous.

Sex and sexuality is the most demonized activity in traditional religion. In Satanism, it is the most glorified. May all parties involved do as they wish. This is not to say that you have to, but if you want to, you should do it as much as you desire.

It is the same with food, drink, music, or any other way you would like to celebrate. It is drilled into us that having too much fun is wrong. Quite the contrary, it is the entire point of being alive. As life serves no particular purpose other than to perpetuate itself, we must all find our own meaning. The meaning of life is whatever you make it. Your mind is the chief intentionality in charge of the world of your subjective experience. Therefore, one must make one's own meaning.

The Satanist also takes great pleasure in doing things in accordance with his or her morality, while simultaneously violating the corrupt, arbitrary morality handed down from earlier cultures and/or imagined deities. Many of the greatest pleasures violate those fallacious moral codes. A Satanist has the pleasure of violating a given, invalid, convention, in addition to the pleasure anyone would derive from the act.

Filling your life and the lives of others around you with as much happiness as you can, and fully indulging for as long as you are able, is a noble pursuit. Everyone must, after all, make the best use of the short time they have.

What is it you enjoy most? What do you like to do? As long as it does not hurt anyone, go for it. Do not let anyone make you feel ashamed about what you enjoy. That is far too much power ever to grant to anyone. Share the things you like with others. This can greatly magnify what you get out of it. Try doing what your friends enjoy. You might find something you did not know about, something you end up deriving a great deal of pleasure from.

This part of the philosophy is almost entirely subjective. It deals with your feelings, and your subjective experience. There is not much that can be right or wrong here—it all depends on your opinions, and how you look at the world. Just remember to make the most of how you experience your life.

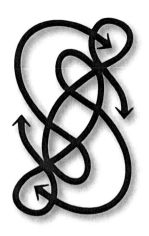

The Narrative of Loki

Loki symbolizes humor, fun, wit, and cunning. Loki is the prankster. Even when working toward serious goals, one cannot be serious all the time. The characteristics of the Loki aspect of Satan can be very useful.

When furthering your activist agenda, you will discover that people notice characteristics of Loki in you. It is just something that tends to shine through and is noticeable. When people see that, they think you are not serious, that you must be trolling, or playing a prank. They do not understand the things you can accomplish with humor.

You can certainly reach goals regarding very serious things through the use of pranks. People tend to think you are not serious, and underestimate you. This makes your cunning and trickery all the more effective if you need to employ it in order to realize a particular goal.

When you examine a situation, you do not look at the way people are misusing it, but rather you look at how you can use it to further your agenda. It will be unexpected, catching people off guard. Keeping things a secret until you are ready to spring it greatly increases the effectiveness of this tactic.

Have plenty of humor in what you do. It makes life more enjoyable for yourself, and those working with you. It also goes over better with the public. People enjoy a good laugh while seeing theocrats and fascists hoist on their own petard.

Just look up the Satanic activism that took place for two to three years leading up to the release of this book. You will see many examples where these elements were employed to great effect. Some activities call for more of that than others do, but they all seem to benefit from this methodology.

The only downside to this is that some people will think your goals are not serious. It is worth it though as these are very effective tactics. People can usually be made to understand what you have achieved as well. Most importantly, skipping the humor would take all the joy out of doing these things——not that they would not still be worthwhile, but you may as well have a good time doing them.

Epilogue

All of these things, which I have detailed, can be combined into one complete philosophy, worldview, and religion. Satan is a metaphorical representation for all of this. I may say to you: "Hail Satan!" That is simply an affirmation of all that I have laid out in this book.

This should easily answer the question of why one would call it Satanism, which is a very common question. Satan symbolizes all this, and therefore it could be called nothing other than "Satanism". Humanism incorporates most of this, but not all. The first two narratives of this book are entirely outside of Humanism. So, if you are this particular variety of Satanist, you are probably many things that are included in what that means, but you are more too.

For example being an atheist is something that all Humanists are, but Humanism is much more specific, with more criteria, and atheism being only part of it. It is the same with this variation of Satanism; it is more specific, with additional criteria, although all aspects of Secular Humanism fit within it. Satanism can encompass one's entire being. Your religion, philosophy, worldview, and even your personality are all contained within this one label.

This is of course, only true of this and similar variations of Satanism. My variation laid out here, The Satanic Temple's variation (which should be nearly identical), and Rational Satanism, are good examples of when this is the case. However, it is not true of any theistic variations or of LaVeyan Satanism, as a counterexample.

I do not go as far as the groups who believe in a sort of Satanic unity, where everyone adopting that label unites. It does not make sense for radically different points of view, some even in diametrical opposition, to have one big love fest and sing Satanic Kumbaya together. I am not into that at all. I also do not like the elitism on the other end of the spectrum though. There is that certain subgroup of LaVeyans who feel there is only one true Satanism. I think that is utter nonsense too.

Those who have read some of my essays written prior to this (posted on Facebook) know exactly what I think about that. Satanism can be anything that is oppositional, adversarial, has the individualism of the Left-Hand Path, and has some sort of a tradition of Satan filling in other aspects of the archetype. Those are the only characteristics definitive of Satanism. Everything else is just characteristics of different variations.

Being that Satanism is so individualistic, as it is of the Left-Hand Path, it is really up to the individual to decide upon identifying with that label. Who really gets to say if one is a true Satanist or not? If you say that you are a Satanist, then a Satanist you are.

The other issue with something so individual is that every person kind of has their own sub-variation. That is those little, subtle differences within a variation. One could certainly make the case that my variation is actually just a sub-variation of The Satanic Temple's. It is true that discovering the organization had a viewpoint identical to my own, at least in all the ways in which their viewpoint was documented, was the primary factor in my joining it. However, there were enough small differences to prompt me to leave and go down my own path. So, the distinction is rather subjective. The same is true of other individuals who belong to other organizations—sometimes even to multiple organizations or Satanic ideologies.

This book contains the details of my own variation of Satanism. However, at no point do I claim it to be the only true Satanism. Instead, I argue the exact opposite. Additionally, part of my variation involves coming up with certain things yourself. My view of Satanism and of the Left-Hand Path is that there must be parts of it left up to the individual as I do here. Your philosophy, worldview, and religion are not in this book—not exactly anyway. Even if you are in total agreement, this book is just the tool of learning, the beginning of your mental journey, of which I am merely a guide. Your philosophy, worldview, and religion actually exist only in one place—your own mind. You are the master of your own subjective experience, through which all of objective reality is filtered. My only hope is that this guides you to where you want to be.

Hail Satan!

About The Author

Damien Ba'al is a Unix/Linux engineer by day and a philosopher by night. He is a Satanist, a skeptic, a critical thinker, and many other things. Damien lives with his wife and cats, where he enjoys a number of intellectual hobbies. He has a love of learning and of teaching. Active on social media, Damien's words convey his dark presence to all the outcasts and individualists traveling the Left-Hand Path.

https://www.facebook.com/author.damien.baal
https://www.facebook.com/atheisticsatanism.org
https://twitter.com/Damien_Baal @Damien_baal
http://atheisticsatanism.com/

CPSIA information can be obtained at www.ICGtesting.com
Printed in the USA
LVOW10s1419130416

483454LV00040B/486/P